Producers and Consumers

William B. Rice

Consultant

Leann Iacuone, M.A.T., NBCT, ATC
Riverside Unified School District

Publishing Credits

Rachelle Cracchiolo, M.S.Ed., *Publisher*
Conni Medina, M.A.Ed., *Managing Editor*
Diana Kenney, M.A.Ed., NBCT, *Senior Editor*
Dona Herweck Rice, *Series Developer*
Robin Erickson, *Multimedia Designer*
Timothy Bradley, *Illustrator*

Image Credits: Cover, p.1 Shutterstock; pp.10, 11
Courtney Patterson; p. 14 Dan Suzio / Science Source;
pp.12, 16, 20, 21, 22 iStock; p.14 Jim Zipp / Science
Source; pp.28, 29 J.J. Rudisill; pp.14, 15 Linda Freshwaters
Arndt / Science Source; p.25 Paul Williams / Alamy; pp.14,
22 Sinclair Stammers / Science Source; pp.22, 23 Timothy
J. Bradley; all other images from Shutterstock.

Library of Congress Cataloging-in-Publication Data

Rice, William B. (William Benjamin), 1961- author.
  Producers and consumers / William B. Rice.
       pages cm
  Summary: "All life is important in its own way. Each
living thing contributes something to our world. Taking
away just one creature can disrupt the delicate balance
nature created. From sprouting plants to crawling
insects to sneaky snakes to vicious cougars--all of these
organisms are intertwined and play a role."-- Provided
by publisher.
  Audience: Grades 4 to 6.
  Includes index.
   ISBN 978-1-4807-4677-0 (pbk.)
 1. Biogeochemical cycles--Juvenile literature. 2. Ecology-
-Juvenile literature. I. Title.
 QH344.R54 2016
 577.1--dc23
                                            2014045244

Teacher Created Materials

5301 Oceanus Drive
Huntington Beach, CA 92649-1030
http://www.tcmpub.com
ISBN 978-1-4807-4677-0

Table of Contents

'Round and 'Round

Earth's cycles are something we can all count on. Winter fades and spring dawns, but we know that winter will come again. Water evaporates into vapor and riverbeds dry, but we know the rain will return. Fires and floods strike, but life will grow anew.

Earth is ever changing. In fact, change is a constant we can count on!

Cycles are a basic part of life. And life on Earth has adapted to cycles and counts on them. The cycle of night and day. The cycle of cold winters and hot summers. The cycle of rest and waking. The cycle of life and death. Cycles are like circles. There is no beginning and no end. A cycle follows a pattern and repeats itself forever. Night follows day follows night follows day follows night. It has been that way since Earth began. And as long as there is an Earth and a sun, it will always be that way.

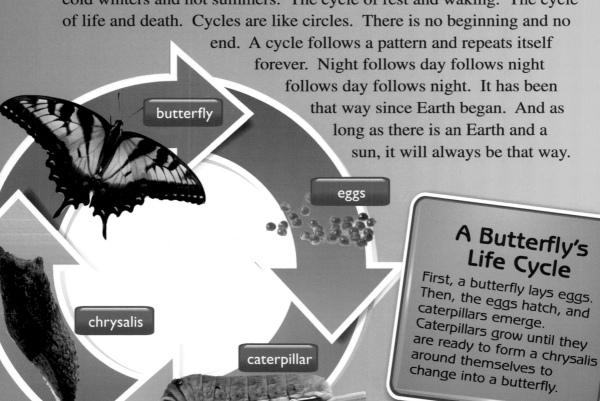

butterfly

eggs

chrysalis

caterpillar

A Butterfly's Life Cycle

First, a butterfly lays eggs. Then, the eggs hatch, and caterpillars emerge. Caterpillars grow until they are ready to form a chrysalis around themselves to change into a butterfly.

How Cycles Work

Cycles keep repeating themselves. To do that, one step must end where the next step begins. Think about cycles in your life. How do you get back to step one?

Each phase of a cycle is **dependent** on the other phases. It counts on the other parts of the cycle. Without them, the phase wouldn't happen. Without spring, there would be no summer. Without the **nutrients** from plants, animals couldn't live. Without animals to nourish the soil, plants would never grow.

The **nutrient cycle** is crucial to all life. It lets matter and **energy** pass among living things. It carries on the flow of life on Earth. The sun is the key. Its energy is the fuel in the cycle. The energy gets passed from one thing to another. It even gets passed to the environment.

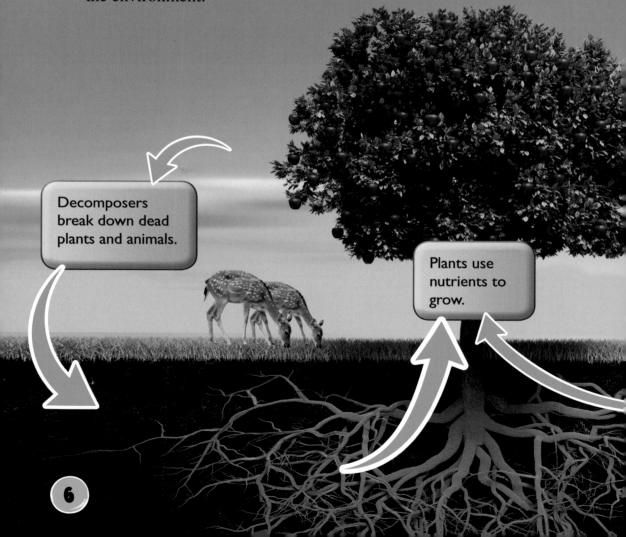

Decomposers break down dead plants and animals.

Plants use nutrients to grow.

Earth's **producers** make food for themselves and for consumers. They make their own food from simple, nonliving substances. Consumers get their nourishment from others. They eat producers and other consumers. Decomposers and producers make use of nutrients from consumers.

Air and water are absorbed into the ground.

Minerals and other nutrients are released into soil.

Rocks break down.

Producers

There's no beginning in a cycle. But for the sake of discussion, we need to start somewhere. So, let's begin with producers.

In the nutrient cycle, producers take basic, nonliving substances and use them to make what they need to grow and live. They make nutrients for themselves. In other words, they make their own food. To do that, they need the sun's energy.

Energy **radiates** outward from the sun every day. Earth receives some of this energy. It makes life on Earth possible. The energy warms the ground. It also warms oceans and lakes. Plants get this energy and use it to help them live. They use this energy to grow. They use it to make their stems and trunks, branches and leaves, and flowers and fruit. They also make their own fuel that powers all this growing.

Since plants produce, or make, their own fuel, they are called *producers*. They make their fuel using energy from the sun.

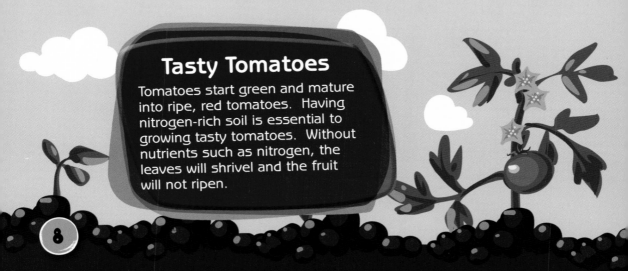

Tasty Tomatoes

Tomatoes start green and mature into ripe, red tomatoes. Having nitrogen-rich soil is essential to growing tasty tomatoes. Without nutrients such as nitrogen, the leaves will shrivel and the fruit will not ripen.

Energy We Use

The sun radiates energy in many forms. Sunlight is the energy we can see. Earth's atmosphere blocks most of the other forms of energy that may be harmful to living things.

A World of Green

The process by which green plants make their own food is called **photosynthesis**. *Photo* means "light." *Synthesis* means "to put together." Photosynthesis puts nutrients together through the use of light.

Light from the sun provides energy for plants. Plants absorb sunlight using **chlorophyll**. It is a chemical found in all green plants. It absorbs light straight from the sun. Chlorophyll mainly absorbs red and blue light. But we see the green light it reflects.

Plants use energy from sunlight to perform photosynthesis. They split hydrogen atoms from water and form new substances. Plants use these substances and carbon dioxide from the air to make glucose.

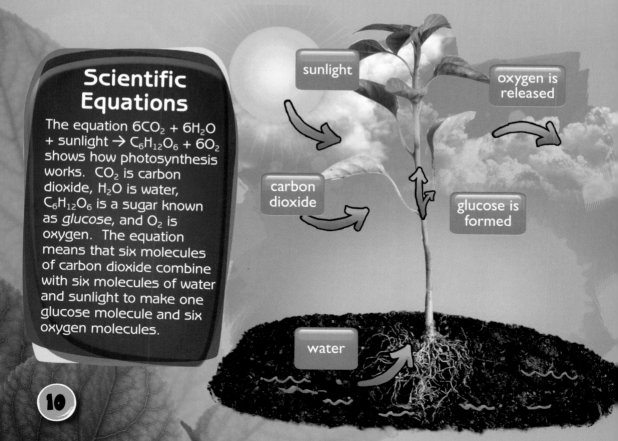

Scientific Equations

The equation $6CO_2 + 6H_2O$ + sunlight $\rightarrow C_6H_{12}O_6 + 6O_2$ shows how photosynthesis works. CO_2 is carbon dioxide, H_2O is water, $C_6H_{12}O_6$ is a sugar known as *glucose*, and O_2 is oxygen. The equation means that six molecules of carbon dioxide combine with six molecules of water and sunlight to make one glucose molecule and six oxygen molecules.

sunlight

oxygen is released

carbon dioxide

glucose is formed

water

Glucose is a simple sugar that all living things need. It has a lot of stored energy. Many of the foods we eat have forms of glucose.

Plants keep glucose in their cells. When they need energy for their living processes, they can use it. Animals consume, or eat, plants and the glucose they contain. Animals use the energy from glucose for *their* living processes.

They Make What?

The new substances plants make are adenosine triphosphate and nicotinamide adenine dinucleotide phosphate hydrogen. Wow! It's a lot easier to call them by their first letters, ATP and NADPH.

Roots and Shoots

When we look at plants, they may seem simple. But with a closer look, there is a lot more to plants than meets the eye. Overall, we can see they are made of two main parts. The part above ground is called the *shoot system*. The shoot system is made of the stem, leaves, flowers, fruits, and seeds. The underground part is called the *root system*.

Roots grow in the dark, moist soil. Shoots grow in the bright, dry air. Plants need the resources from each of these different environments.

Plants use shoot systems to get sunlight and carbon dioxide from the air. They use root systems to get water and minerals from the soil. The sun provides the energy that plants need to make food, cells, and **tissues**.

Different Roots

Not all roots are the same. There are two main kinds of root systems.

Fibrous root systems have many roots about the same size that are spread out with smaller roots coming off these larger roots.

Taproot systems have one big main root going down deep into the soil with several smaller roots coming off the main root.

Studying Systems
Water, soil, and nutrients are absorbed and flow through different parts of plants.

leaf

flower

fruit

shoot system

stem

root system

roots

13

Connection to Consumers

Many animals eat different parts of plants. Some animals eat fruits and nuts. Others eat leaves and stems. Some animals drink the nectar from flowers.

Luckily, plants can regrow and replenish these plant parts. But why would plants let animals eat their parts in the first place? Wouldn't they develop some form of protection to make them stop? The truth is, when animals eat these different plant parts, they actually help the plants. Here's how.

Scat Attack

Animal poop, or scat, is recognizable by its shape. The shape depends on what the animal eats.

Animals that eat only plants usually have smaller, pellet-shaped scat made out of ground plants.

Animals that eat only animals usually have scat with tapered ends and fur or feathers inside of it.

Animals that eat plants and other animals have scat of all different shapes and sizes.

When animals drink nectar, they often spread flower pollen from one flower to the next. This fertilizes the flowers and helps plants make seeds.

Animals also help plants by eating their fruit. Fruits have seeds inside. When animals eat the fruit, they drop some seeds on the ground. The seeds then grow to make new plants.

Finally, by eating leaves and stems, animals process plant substances in their bodies. When they are finished with these substances, they get rid of them. How? They poop them onto the ground. There, the poop is turned back into basic substances by decomposers. Then, plants take these basic substances back up through their roots. The cycle goes on.

Getting Energy

Animals can't use energy straight from the sun like plants can. They can't make the basic materials their bodies need. They don't use the sun's energy to power what their bodies need to do—breathe, move, and release waste.

As we know, plants store energy in their parts. They also have nutrients. Many animals must eat plants to stay alive. They use plant materials for growing and taking care of their own bodies. This process of eating plants for their nutrients is called **consumption**. The animals are consumers. They consume their nutrients. All animals are consumers, including humans.

Animals need nutrients to grow and keep their body tissues healthy. Nutrients are available in many forms. Animals have developed different methods for getting those nutrients. But there are two main ways that animals do this. Both involve eating.

Food Webs

All living things are interconnected. If you draw a picture to show how different plants and animals depend on one another for energy and nutrients, it might look like a spiderweb. Because of this, many people use the term *food web* to describe these relationships. Food webs show how energy moves through an ecosystem.

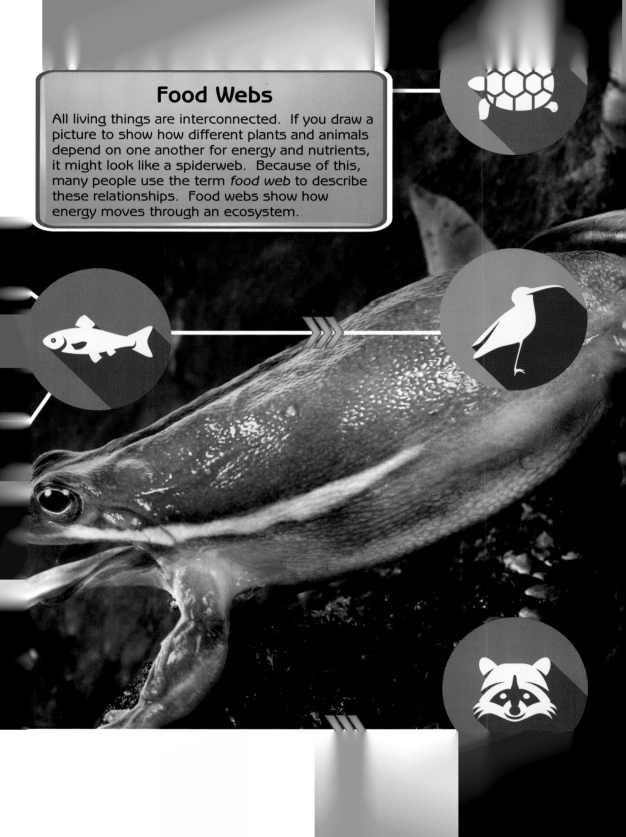

Types of Consumers

One way animals get their nutrients is by eating different parts of plants. These animals are called **herbivores**. Herbivores may eat roots, stems, leaves, fruits, flowers, nectar, or seeds. Every animal has its preferences. Some eat the entire plant!

The other way for animals to get nutrients is by eating other animals. These animals are called **carnivores**. They are meat eaters. These animals mainly hunt and kill their prey. But some carnivores eat meat that has been killed by other animals or that dies naturally. These animals are **scavengers**.

Many animals actually use both ways to get their nutrients. They eat plants and they eat other animals. These animals are called **omnivores**.

Humans are animals. Which type of consumer are we? We eat plants such as carrots, peas, broccoli, and corn. We can also eat many kinds of meats such as chicken, fish, pork, and beef. Since we eat plants and animals, we are omnivores. Other omnivores include bears, pigs, dogs, foxes, and badgers.

Zebras have strong front teeth for biting grass and other plants.

Teeth Are Tools

Herbivores, carnivores, and omnivores can be recognized by their teeth. What kind of teeth do you have?

deer

hedgehog

Herbivores have broad, flat teeth that help them grind plants

Omnivores have a variety of sharp and flat teeth to help them eat plants and animals.

Carnivores have long, sharp teeth that help them rip, tear, and cut through prey.

tiger

Flow of Energy

Energy flows from the sun to plants. Energy and nutrients flow from plants to animals. Energy and nutrients flow between animals, too.

All organisms have a life cycle. They are born, they grow, they live, they produce offspring, and over time, they die. What happens to their bodies when they die? They **decompose**, or break down. But they don't decompose on their own. Scavengers and decomposers help the process along.

A Putrid Party

Animals decompose a little differently than plants do. While plant decomposition is relatively easy to watch, animal decomposition can look more like a horror movie. Scavengers such as vultures and insects such as maggots all join in.

Vultures pick at the remains of a dead animal.

Maggots devour a dead salmon.

A common word for decomposing is *rotting*.

No single type of organism can decompose a dead organism on its own. Scavengers often start the process. Then, decomposers such as bacteria and fungi, finish the job. They each act on certain parts of an organism at varying times.

Imagine what would happen if decomposers didn't act on dead organisms. Earth would be covered with dead plants and animals! All the nutrients would be locked up in the bodies of these dead organisms. If that were true, no new life could be produced.

Decomposition

Plants are made of individual cells. The cell walls are made of a strong substance called *cellulose*. Lignin is another substance that is found mainly in the cells of plants. Some parts of dead plants and animals take longer to decompose than others do. Fats, sugars, and proteins are decomposed easily and quickly. However, substances such as plant cellulose, lignin, shells, and animal bones decompose very slowly.

Humus is found in every ecosystem. It's made from living things that have died. It's made of the parts that have resisted normal decomposition. These parts have reached a point of **stability**. Humus will not easily break down any further. It's an important part of soil. It helps the soil maintain moisture and nutrients.

There are four key stages of decomposition. First, there is leaching. That is the process by which minerals are taken from something solid and dissolved into liquids. Second, the solid starts to break apart as it releases the dissolved matter. Third, humus is produced. Finally, the humus takes a form that plants can use for nutrients.

humus

Watch your spelling. *Hummus* is a tasty treat. *Humus*...not so much!

Standing Tall

Hemicellulose is similar to cellulose, but with a different internal structure. It helps form the strength of the cell wall.

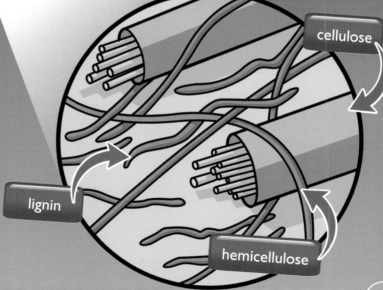

cell wall

cellulose

lignin

hemicellulose

Decomposers help living things by breaking down dead plants and animals. They make important nutrients for living plants to use. Decomposers also use the products of their work and the energy from dead things for their own processes. They're decomposers and consumers. Bacteria, fungi, insects, and some other types of animals are all decomposers.

Bacteria are single-celled organisms. They can be found in soil. Some bacteria make geosmin. It's a substance with a very "earthy" smell. It's what gives the air that certain smell after it rains following a long dry period. When you smell it, you know that decomposition is at work.

Fungi are special types of organisms. They include mold, yeast, and mushrooms. Mushrooms are really the fruit of a soil organism called *mycelia*. Mycelia can be very small. Or they can spread out over a large area.

Earthworms are common decomposers. They eat their way through soil. They leave behind soil that is rich in nutrients. This makes healthy and strong soil for plants to grow.

mushrooms

The smell of fir trees that so many people enjoy is actually the smell of decomposition.

Brown Belt Beauties

Bacteria, fungi, and earthworms are key decomposers. They form the lower "brown-belt" layer of ecosystems in soil. They consume dirt particles and break them down into even smaller sizes so plants can use the nutrients.

Our Role

Every human plays a role in the nutrient cycle. Our role may be even more important than we think! More than any other living thing, humans impact the entire cycle in big ways.

Being aware of our environment enhances our enjoyment of life. It also shapes how well we survive and thrive. Understanding our place as a consumer in the nutrient cycle is part of this awareness. Our actions affect the world around us every day. Healthy choices help to support a healthy environment. And a healthy environment supports our health, too!

The more we're aware of the effects of our choices, the wiser our choices will be. As consumers who can think and reason, we must develop our ability to see the world as it is. After all, this is what science is all about!

Think Like a Scientist

What's the best way to help food decompose? Experiment and find out!

What to Get

- 3 clear jars
- food
- grass and leaves
- marker
- soil
- trash, such as plastic bottle tops
- water
- worms

What to Do

1 Fill each jar with about two inches of moist soil. Label the first jar *compost*, the second jar *trash*, and the third jar *worms*.

2 In the jars labeled *compost* and *worms*, place one layer of small pieces of food on top of the soil, then a layer of leaves, and a layer of grass on top.

3 In the jar labeled *trash*, layer small pieces of trash on top of the soil.

4 In the jar labeled *worms*, place worms on top of the grass pieces.

5 Leave the jars open on a windowsill for two weeks. Observe the jars every few days and record your observations on a chart like the one below. Make sure to give your jars a little water once a week. What changes do you see? How are the materials in the jars similar and different?

	Compost Jar	Worm Jar	Trash Jar
Monday			
Wednesday			
Friday			

Glossary

carnivores—living things that eat meat

chlorophyll—the green substance in plants that makes it possible for them to make glucose from carbon dioxide

consumption—the act of eating or drinking something

decompose—to slowly break down

dependent—decided or controlled by something else

energy—power that can be used to do something

herbivores—living things that eat plants

nutrient cycle—the movement or exchange of substances that living things need to grow

nutrients—substances that living things need to grow

omnivores—living things that eat both meat and plants

photosynthesis—the process in which plants use sunlight to combine water and carbon dioxide to make their own food (glucose)

producers—living things that make their own food

radiates—sends out energy in the form of rays or waves

scavengers—animals that feed on dead or decaying animals

stability—the quality or state of something that is not easily changed or likely to change

tissues—materials that form the parts of plants or animals

Index

Your Turn!

Signs of Decomposition

Pick a spot outdoors and look around. What signs do you see of decomposing life? What does it look like? What does it smell like? Is it letting off heat? See how many signs of decomposition you can find.